What Every Woman Needs to Know About Meditation

The Truth of How Meditation Can Bring Peace to Your Life

By Olivia Connors

Editor Sherilyn Raemer

Alternative Imaginings Press

Introduction – Why You Should Read This Book

We are living in a world full of stress, pollutants, and spiritual poverty. Money seems to be one of the most important goals of life today and in its pursuit most people lose all else – mental peace, health, love, family, and spirituality.

It is not surprising that the global rate of suicide has increased by 60 percent over the past 45 years. Think about it: This rate indicates that every 40 seconds someone commits suicide in the world.

Why do you think this is happening? Why do you think people lose faith in living? Then, there are the many, who don't choose to end their lives, but struggle with life while under a great deal of stress.

Women, when compared to men, often bear twice the burden with modernization. Once upon a time, the roles of a man and women were clearly identified. The man was the provider and the woman the homemaker. Each one had to focus on just one aspect of building the family. Today, the roles of men and women, merge into a murky grey color. Both partners need to find time to build their career as well as take care of their family.

Earlier, women were the center of the home. Women were responsible for seeing that her family was looked after and comfortable in every aspect. Gradually, added to the role of homemaker was the role of bread winner, contributing to the family income by working shoulder to shoulder with men.

Having a career and homemaking are both full time jobs. To be good at both, women need to work doubly as hard as men in both areas. This put tremendous stress on their minds and bodies.

It gets you thinking. Is there a way out? Is it possible to live in this world and yet, not allow it to affect you so much that you are overwhelmed by negative emotions? Is there any means to calm the mind and refocus energy toward a positive outcome, whenever stress causes negative emotions to peak?

The answer to all of these questions is, "YES."

Yes, you can manage any type of stress and still function normally and productively with the right tool - meditation.

Meditation is the means to calm your mind and provide you with inner peace, and it will help you cope with the terrible onslaught of stress that the modern world throws at you.

This book focuses on the benefits of meditation for women, but with the exception of a few instances, men stand to benefit just as much from meditation as women do.

You will find the Table of Contents next, which gives you a solid idea of just what you are going to find covered here.

Table of Contents

INTRODUCTION – WHY YOU SHOULD READ THIS BOOK

CHAPTER 1: WHAT IS MEDITATION?

- MEDITATION: THE BASICS
- HOW MEDITATION WORKS
  - *Beta waves*
  - *Alpha waves*
  - *Theta waves*
  - *Delta waves*
  - *Gamma waves*
- DOES MEDITATION REALLY HELP?
  - *Blushing*
  - *Hypertension and Heart Attack*
  - *Fainting*
  - *Vomiting and Nausea*
  - *Migraine*
  - *Wet Dreams*
- THE BENEFITS OF MEDITATION FOR WOMEN
  - *The Physical Benefits of Meditation*
  - *The Psychological Benefits of Meditation*
  - *The Spiritual Benefits of Meditation*
  - *Meditation and Happiness*
  - *Meditation Success and Prosperity*
  - *Meditation and Grief*

CHAPTER 2 - WHAT MEDITATION IS NOT - 7 MEDITATION MYTHS EXPLODED

- *Myth 1: You Have to Be Religious to Start Meditating*
- *Myth 2: Meditation Is Just a Form of Relaxation*
- *Myth 3: Meditation and Self-Hypnosis Are The Same*
- *Myth 4: Meditation Can Be 'Fast Forwarded'*
- *Myth 5: Meditation Needs You to Take the Lotus Position*
- *Myth 6: Meditation Is For Escapists*
- *Myth 7: If You Don't Do It Every Day It's Not Worth the Trouble*

CHAPTER 3 - 8 TYPES OF MEDITATION

#1 Zazen (Buddhist meditation) Or Zen Meditation
   The Zazen Method
#2 Yoga Meditation (Any Type)
#3 Vipassana
#4 Taoist – The Chinese Meditation
#5 Qigong
#6 Mantra
#7 Metta Meditation or Loving-Kindness Meditation
#8 Guided Meditation

CHAPTER 4 - THE STARTING POINT OF MEDITATION

Visions
Hearing Things
Sudden Fears
9 Quick Tips For Beginners
   Expect Trouble, Be Prepared
Find a Position That You Find Comfortable
Use the Stop Watch
Start With Rhythmic Breathing
Use Visualization Whenever You Can
Use Noting When You Feel Lost
Yoga for Body and Mind Relaxation
   Aim Low and Achieve High
Get Into a Habit Groove
Meditation Tools
Music
   Sound
   Candle
   Light

CHAPTER 5 - YOGA AND MEDITATION

Yoga – What is this?
   Yama or the 5 Abstentions
   Niyama or the 5 Observances
   Asana
   Pranayama or Breathing
   Pratyahara or Abstraction
   Dharana Od Concentrration

    Dhyana Or Meditation
    Samadhi or Liberation
  THE IMPORTANCE OF YOGA IN MEDITATION
    Does Yoga Meditation Change Brain Activity?

MOVING FORWARD FROM HERE

COPYRIGHT

DISCLAIMER:

Chapter 1: What is Meditation?

Meditation: The Basics

In spite of the popularity of the term, very few actually understand what meditation is. For most people, this is still a mystic thing that people from the Orient have mastered.

Meditation is a heightened level of awareness where the mind is still. To get there takes years of practice, sometimes a lifetime. This isn't shared to scare you away; quite the opposite. It is pointed out so you can understand what meditation is so you aren't disappointed with how it progresses.

Most people introduce meditation into their life and then drop it because they feel they cannot do it. This happens because their perception about meditation is wrong.

It is common to confuse the *"state of meditation"* with the *"path to meditation."* The key to success is to stop focusing on the results, and start concentrating on the process. Simply put, it's taking one step at a time. Or, as meditation will teach you, living in the present 100 percent.

Stop thinking about reaching that blissful realm, where you are one with the Universe, and start focusing on the path that takes you there. It is true that the state of enlightenment is totally achievable and everyone has the ability to achieve it, but it takes a long time and serious effort that for some translates into many years of concentrated effort to get there.

In this book we are not talking here about renouncing the world and leading an ascetic's life while pursuing enlightenment. We are focused on teaching you methods to calm the mind through meditation to ensure that stress no longer affects your health and mental wellbeing.

How Meditation Works

A lot has been written about meditation and many have their own ideas about it. It looks like civilization has come full circle with the developments and understanding of meditation today.

In ancient times, ascetics of India, Egypt, China, and Japan respected the power of meditation. At that time, science was frowned upon, and often considered anti-religion, anti-God and anti-human.

As civilizations underwent 'modernization' the line between science and religious beliefs crossed and gradually science became the Word and Truth, while religion and things like meditation, which pointed to the hidden powers of the mind and nature, were pushed into the background.

Mediation has been the focus of plenty of scientific research, and the findings of the majority of these studies are amazing. Once upon a time, it was believed that every person was born with a basic intelligence that rarely could be improved during one life's time. You could gain knowledge and skills, but intelligence would remain at the same level.

Now science has started appreciating some of the facts that our ancestors knew: you can change the brain structure and your mental ability with a certain amount of training. Meditation is one such method that can enhance the capacity of the brain exponentially.

When studies were carried out on the brain activity of Buddhist monks and compared to that of novices during meditation, it was found that the gamma wave' activity in the brain of the monks was extremely elevated, while in the novices it was hardly noticeable. In order to explain this more vividly, you could compare the impact of meditation on the brain with what bodybuilding exercises do for the body.

It is common knowledge today that the brain projects electro-magnetic activity. The waves generated by the brain correspond with one's mental and physical state.

The consciousness can be divided into four distinct brain stages, each one determined by the waves that dominate the activity of the brain at any given time.

For example, if beta waves are most prominent, then the brain is said to be in beta stage, if alpha waves dominate, the brain would be classified at being in an alpha state and so on.

Beta waves

When you use your brain extensively, like when you are solving a difficult math problem, your brain manifests these waves. Their frequency range is 15-30 Hz and beta waves represent the completely awake and alert state of mind. When these waves are found during meditation, they indicate a high level of meditation experience and a mental state of the highest concentration and ecstasy.

Alpha waves

These waves indicate a state of tranquility, happiness, and relaxation. The alpha waves are usually found during a meditative state of mind and their range is 9-15 Hz. Outside meditation, you will find alpha waves in the period just-before-falling-asleep or in connection with marijuana (cannabis) use. The high given by this drug is similar to the floating feeling that you experience before you fall asleep.

Theta waves

These waves are found during the "twilight state," like when you lose the feeling that you are lying down waiting to sleep, but you are not yet fully asleep. The consciousness is reduced to such a level where you are neither awake nor asleep.

You will also find these waves when you are under hypnosis, deep meditation, and also when you are having a reality based dream. In many cases, you would find solutions to your problems during this stage, or be inspired to do work differently. The frequency range of the waves is 4-8 Hz.

Delta waves

These waves are found during the deepest stage of your sleep. There are no dreams in this stage, only the deepest level of unconsciousness.

The frequency range of these waves is very low, 1-3 Hz. It is possible to bring your mind to this state through meditation; in such a case you would dead to the world as every sensation in the body would be minimized including your heartbeat, respiration, and other vital signs.

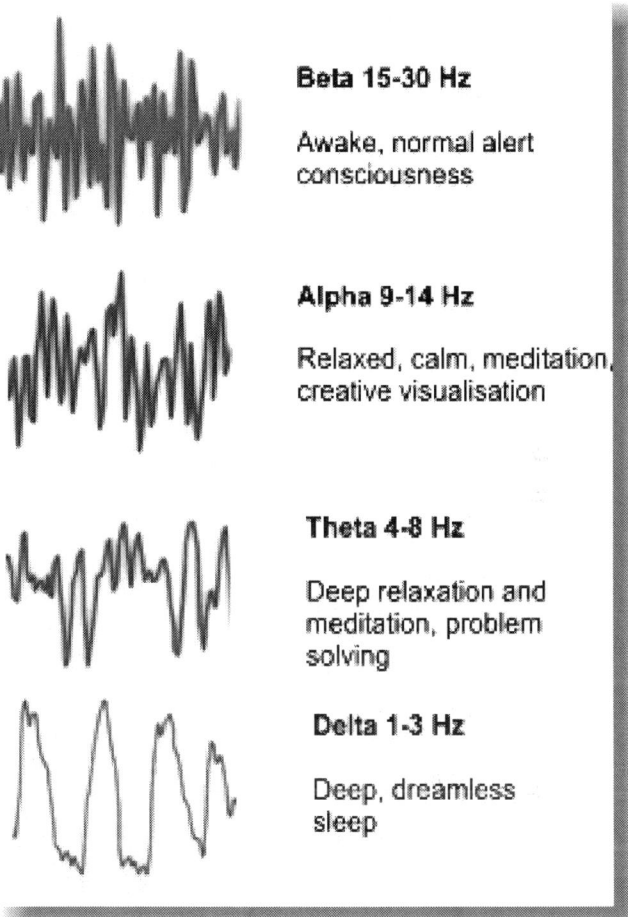

Gamma waves

These waves are found in frequencies of 30-70 Hz and they are associated with audio-visual and tactile feelings. You will find these waves during meditation and/or listening to peaceful music.

These brain waves cannot exist in isolation like the other types of waves; they have to be associated with the beta, alpha, theta, or delta waves. This is why there is no gamma stage of brain.

You will find these waves during meditation where self-induced imagination plays a large role; the person is awake yet feels and visualizes things that are imposed on the mind.

During meditation, there is a very gradual transition from the highest frequency waves in the brain to the lowest possible frequencies. The novice has to walk through the stages to reach the ultimate goal of delta waves through meditation, while an experienced practitioner can invoke the stage at will.

As a matter of fact, martial arts masters can control their mind with the same effectiveness as a meditation master, which implies that the brain stages can be achieved through mind control and training.

Meditation is used as a vehicle to reach the ultimate state of bliss where the mind experiences the highest form of ecstasy. Monks explain it as *"becoming enlightened"* or *"becoming one with the Universe."*

Science tried to replicate this through hypnosis, and to a large extent, they were successful, though you cannot really say that a hypnotized person would benefit mentally as much as one would do from meditation.

Science is still looking for a way to achieve the meditation stage of brain through direct stimulus, but they have not had much of a breakthrough. It is possible to fast-forward a few steps in the meditation ladder, but a shortcut has not yet been found.

Does Meditation Really Help?

Why meditate? Does meditation really help? Why is this exercise quoted as a benefit to modern civilization? Why is the medical fraternity more and more interested in understanding the intricacies of this process, and the impact it has on the health of the mind and body? These are a few of the questions that you may have, if you are considering adding meditation to your life.

The core of the answers to all of these questions is that it relaxes, period. In this day and age, when everything from being a homemaker to building a career adds heavily to your stress levels, meditation brings a calmness and stability that cannot be compared to anything else. This relaxation not only helps keep your mind cool and focused; it also improves your health.

You will find that people who meditate are kinder and more empathic towards the less fortunate in society. Meditation helps in opening the mind to other people's suffering. This is why you often find that those who are heavily involved in their local communities are exceptionally skilled at meditation.

Meditation sharpens your focus on your purpose in life. Off hand, if someone asked you what your purpose in life is, what would be your answer? The most common answer would be to be successful financially, professionally, and personally. How many people do you think would answer, "*To find out who I am in reality*"?

Now, unless you know who you are in the big picture, how do you really focus on the purpose of your life? How do you identify this? Meditation bridges the worldly realm with the spiritual realm, giving you the whole picture from within. The realization is so fulfilling and satisfying that it would make you realize how futile it is to run after the "good things" of this life, when the real gold is elsewhere.

Meditation lowers your blood pressure, controls pain, calms your nerves, improves your memory and concentration, makes you more patient and emphatic, treats gastric and digestive problems, controls heart problems and so much more. The list is much longer than this, which makes you wonder whether the mind can exercise so much power.

Does it really have such an immense capacity? Yes, it does. If you want immediate proof, you do not need to read studies; just take a look at things that are common in your life:

Blushing

Somebody pays you a compliment and you blush with embarrassment. You are caught doing something wrong, and your cheeks turn red with embarrassment. You might also blush with pleasure.

Hypertension and Heart Attack

You are provoked to anger, and you find yourself with heart palpitations, chest pain, seeing black in front of your eyes, while your cheeks, ears and neck turn fiery red. These are symptoms of acute anger.

Fainting

You see someone you love getting badly hurt and you faint. Even if you were not the over-sensitive type, you would still feel faint because of the empathy that is instantly created.

Vomiting and Nausea

You see a gruesome murder or you witness the butchering of a chicken, and you have the urge to throw up.

Migraine

You have an argument with someone and it upsets you thoroughly. You end up with a migraine headache.

Wet Dreams

Both men and women can experience orgasm while sleeping. You dreamt about a sexual encounter, and you experience a full-fledged orgasm. How is that possible without any physical stimulation?

These examples are just a few examples that prove beyond a doubt that your mind has tremendous influence over your body.

Meditation is the process by which you can regulate, control, and use the power of your mind to achieve anything in your life. Worth trying, right?

The Benefits of Meditation For Women

The benefits of meditations are immense. They affect every aspect of your wellbeing – mental, physical, and spiritual. People who have practiced meditation over the years have acquired the ability to stay calm in times of crisis, enjoy better relationships with the people they love and with their coworkers, enjoy better health, and feel more connected with the Universe at large.

In the 21st Century, meditation has indeed been rediscovered when it comes to health, longevity, and natural healing. It is a well-known fact that Mother Nature left to its own devices, has the most intricate way to balance itself. Unfortunately, humans while searching for ways to improve on this balance actually managed to push it into an abyss of imbalance.

The result has been catastrophic. Humans have engineered a path towards sure self-destruction, which is exceptionally camouflaged by promises for additional comforts in life. In their quest for *"more and better,"* they are getting *"less and worse."*

Meditation is an antidote that can counter this effect and return the reins of life into the hands of Nature. In other words, meditation has the ability to make your life better. This has been proven by numerous scientific studies.

The Physical Benefits of Meditation

This is easy to prove. There are numerous physical benefits that meditation brings into your life. In fact, it is these very obvious benefits that compelled the medical profession to take notice, research meditation, and lastly accept it as one of the most powerful self-remedial measures the human body can utilize.

Meditation Reverses Stress-Related Symptoms

As a woman, you are no stranger to stress, and often quite helpless in its path. You cannot exclude stress from your life, but you can prevent it from harming you, and you can also reverse the impact it has already had on you. This is one of the most important things that meditation can do for you.

In a study conducted by the Harvard Medical School, the brain was closely monitored to map the activity that takes place during meditation. The results pointed to the fact that meditation fires those sections of the brain that are responsible for the autonomic nervous system such as blood pressure, ovulation, and digestion, among others.

These are exactly the areas in the body that stress has a negative effect on. This explains why people who practice meditation feel better with time; the meditation counters the effect of the stress on the autonomic nervous system, putting things back in order.

Meditation Boosts Your Immune System

Meditation also strengthens the body from within empowering it to defend itself against minor and major infections. Yoga meditation has asanas (postures) that can even help to combat cancer. Ascetics from ancient India, Zen masters of Japan, and the Chinese Masters practicing Tai Chi could keep their bodies disease-free, even in the most hostile environments, with nothing less than bare necessities for nourishment. This is the power of meditation.

Meditation Manages Pain Effectively

Psychomatic Medicine published a paper on the study of the impact of meditation on cancer patients. Just seven weeks of meditation was able to bring down pain, anxiety, and anger, in these patients. Amazing, is it not?

Meditation Improves Brain Function

Meditation has the ability to counter the effects of diseases such as Alzheimer's, Parkinson's, and dementia, etc. When meditating, the brain is in a constant flux. In fact, there are studies that prove conclusively that meditation actively promotes regeneration of brain cells. Age-related memory loss and malfunction can be reversed through meditation because it keeps the brain working.

The Psychological Benefits of Meditation

From the above it is clear that meditation does impact your health in very tangible ways. You can see the difference between how you feel before and after meditation.

Most people who start practicing meditation *"just to see how it is,"* and then they find that they are unable to stop because they love the *"special high"* they get from it. That *'special high'* is the result of charging the brain – literally.

The psychological benefits are more subtle, and therefore, a little difficult to identify and isolate. That meditation reduces anxiety, and induces calm and tranquility, is beyond debate.

It has also been proven that the control it has over anxiety is very beneficial in depression treatments. Let us look at what research has proven. Here are some of the things that are widely accepted today about meditation and its impact on the psyche:

Meditation Increases Tolerance

Women who meditate find that they become more tolerant in all aspects of their lives: children, spouse, boss, traffic jams, plans that fall apart, frustration, and so on. People who meditate also find it easier to handle monotony in their jobs (when these involve repetitive activities); they are able to stay with the job in spite of it being boring and uninspiring.

Meditation Increases Concentration and Attention

Women who practice meditation find that they are able to concentrate better – whether they are studying, doing household chores, working in a job, or just reading the newspaper. Meditation makes their minds alert, ready to assimilate details and ready to act.

Meditation Enhances Memory and Intelligence

Meditation improves the capacity of the brain to retain and recall information. This is not only a major boon in day-to-day life, but also excellent news for those at high risk for Alzheimer's and similar mind-degenerative diseases.

In fact, millions of dollars are being pumped into research that is looking at the possibility of using this method for prevention, and for reversing mind deterioration.

It has been proven through various studies that the brain is rejuvenated and strengthened through meditation. Studies show that people who practice meditation on a daily basis perform better on intelligence tests.

Meditation Decreases Mental Stress Levels

A hormone known as *"cortisol"* inundates your blood stream when you are stressed, causing your body's systems to go awry. This hormone is responsible for the activation of the flight-or-fight response of the body, which is also known as the *"emergency or survival mode"*.

In this mode, all the non-critical systems in the body are put on hold, such as your digestive system, reproductive system, immune system, lymphatic system, urinary system, and endocrine system.

This is why women who are stressed over a prolonged period of time, develop various health problems – infertility, digestive problems, urinary infections, repetitive infection and hormonal imbalance.

Also, cortisol is the hormone that causes extreme cravings for food, which when turned into the fat gets deposited in the abdomen region.

Meditation controls cortisol and one other stress related ingredient in your blood stream – lactate. This is the compound, that when produced in excess causes anxiety.

Meditation Increases Empathy

Studies have shown that people who meditate have a heightened empathy level (Sweet and Johnson, 1990).

This is in harmony with the fact that meditation equalizes people by increasing their ability to tolerate, feel for others, and interchange places with them.

There is less "*I*" (ego) in the mind of people who meditate, and therefore they are more open to the world, their surroundings, and the eople around them.

Meditation Increases Creativity and Self-Actualization

Meditation is for the brain what exercise is for the body. In other words, meditation helps the brain think better and perform better.

This is why meditation is shown to improve creative skills, perception, self-actualization, and personal development as a whole. The person who regularly meditates is confident but not snobbish; self-assured but not condescending; mentally reactive but not impulsive.

Meditation is particularly powerful at improving verbal proficiency and originality, along with increasing sensory experiences, and visualization. People who meditate exhibit high self-esteem and maturity; they show a significant merging of their ideal social being and self.

Meditation Increased Auto-Hypnotic Suggestibility

Meditation is highly dependent on your ability to concentrate. It comes as no surprise that it helps increase your auto-hypnotic suggestibility. You are able to literally tell your body what to do.

Monks and masters who regularly meditate deeply, develop the ability to lower or raise their heartbeat, blood pressure, brain activity and other involuntary activities in their body; all, by means of concentration.

Of course, this is an advanced level of meditation skills, but even at the beginner levels, you can influence your mind to positive thinking and through it to a more fulfilling day-to-day life.

Meditation Reversal and Control of Depression

Meditation clearly is able to reverse depression by controlling anxiety and stress induced signals to the body's systems.

People who meditate regularly find it easier to maintain their cool, even in extremely trying circumstances.

Experiments showed that even a mere 15 minutes of meditation per day can reduce anxiety and reverse depression. That's pretty incredible!

Meditation Prevents and Counters Addictions

Meditation is excellent for countering all types of addictions and neurosis by simply stabilizing the mind sufficiently not to need anything extra.

Since meditation helps you to better understand yourself and increases your self-regard and self-esteem, you will feel on the top of the world, and no longer need any other type of *"high."*

Meditation Counters Psychosomatic Diseases

Disorders such as insomnia, migraines, hysteria, others that are mostly triggered by anxiety and depression are easily countered using meditation.

In fact, many studies indicate that meditation is a far better treatment for such disorders than hypnosis, considering that hypnosis is externally induced, while meditation is self-controlled.

The Spiritual Benefits of Meditation

Meditation was first identified as an integral part of religion, spiritualism, and a quest to know the truth. Every religion has its own version, but at the core it is the same:

- *"Dhyana"* is the word for *"meditation"* in Sanskrit, which literally means *"contemplation"*. The transcendental meditation or TM as it referred to in scientific studies originates from the Vedas as conceptualized by the Maharishi Mahesh Yogi.

- The I Ching (The Book of Changes) forms the basis of meditation in China. The roots of meditation in both these cases are separate, and religious based. Then we have the Buddhist monks, whom the modern science owes so much to for helping to understand meditation and its impact on the human psyche, who are once again governed by religion.

- His Holiness the Dalai Lama, who is also the winner of 1989 Nobel Prize for Peace, has indicated that meditation may be the only path to learn the truth and be immersed into it.

- In Christian connotation, meditation is intricately tied up with spiritual awakening.

Wherever you look, you will find that in the past meditation has been a journey towards a religious destination. Its application and adaptation to the modern world is very recent, say over the last two decades at best.

Before that, meditation was more associated with the search for Universal Truth, understanding religious doctrines, seeking the path to enlightenment, and the like.

All other benefits were a bonus that came with adopting meditation as a path towards this quest. However, today meditation is often practiced with no link to religion, but rather to spirituality.

Meditation as a Coping Mechanism

Meditation is not only a form of quieting the babble that constantly goes on in your mind, but also a way to realize that as humans we are capable of and meant for bigger things than mere existence.

Every day we look for answers to questions in our lives; things that do not make sense; things that we do not understand; things that we do not deserve. Meditation helps us find the answers, accept ourselves for who we are, and raise ourselves beyond mere animal-level existence.

At some time in your life, you will have fallen prey to something that you find acutely unfair, such as losing your job; or having someone close to you suddenly die.

When you are faced with such things, it is very hard to deal with the sense of loss and grief that assaults your heart and mind. Sometimes, the sadness and feelings of hopelessness turn into anger, even rage, which consume you from inside, and could lead you on a path of self-destruction.

Meditation as an Emotional Anchor

The Universe is watching out for you and protecting you at all times. This is a very important for you to realize, because it not only gives you the security and strength to face life, it also keeps your mind from over-reacting to excess joy or sorrow.

Meditation connects you with the Universe, Law of Attraction, God, the Great Design, and other such things that balance good and evil in the world. Most of us agree that there is a higher power that keeps the world in balance.

Without such a belief, life would suddenly lose all meaning and logic. You would be tempted to end your life at the first serious incident in your life that upsets you; or you would lose your sanity because of the pain and frustration these incidents cause you. The fact that they can make you distraught.

Meditation helps you look inside yourself and understand the Universe better. This one simple sentence encompasses the whole essence of a human being's life. It gives direction, the ability to cope and it connects people. Meditation facilitates empathy towards your fellow beings because you see yourself in them.

You realize that you are a part of a whole made up of all the human beings on the plant. It makes you empathize with what is happening around you. *"Do unto others, as you would want others do unto you"* is not a mere statement. It is the philosophy of life that even though it is well known, is internalized by only a few. When you internalize it, it changes you from the inside, and it makes you a better person; a person who can find joy in giving as much as in receiving.

Meditation Provides a Moral Compass

There are a few things that are seen as inherently bad and others as inherently good. Who makes the rules? How do you decide what is good and what is bad? What are the yardsticks used and by whom? The answer is simple. You decide whether you want to follow a societal indict or not, based on your inner moral compass.

You might not immediately fight a wrong or oppose it, but you will definitely have a gut-feeling (some call it conscience) telling you whether you feel it is right or wrong. That yardstick is personal and based upon your understanding of the balance of the Universe, the existence of a God or Power bigger than ourselves, the ability of the world to right itself, and your ability to empathize with others.

Meditation provides an inner moral compass as you start looking inside yourself for peace. The better you know yourself, the more in touch you are with your conscience, the clearer it becomes what is wrong or right according to your core values.

Meditation as an Anti-Aging Tool

Aging is a phenomenon that all living things are subjected to; everyone who is born will one day die. However, human beings have, since time immemorial, endeavored to conquer death and retain their youth and vitality throughout their lives. Unfortunately, the quest is still going on.

It is believed that women are more obsessed with their appearance than men are. Actually, both genders readily qualify their own personal worth by the way they are perceived by their peers.

This is why aging is one of the most depressing aspects in the life of a human. Meditation can slow down the clock quite significantly. It can also reverse the ravages of aging on the face, body, mind, and health.

How can something as simple as mental relaxation stop aging? In ancient days, yogis (ascetics who practiced yoga in India) lived for hundreds of years without aging a bit. This is recorded in the Vedas, but it is often referred to as Hindu legends. The same *"legends"* are recorded informally in China, Japan, and Egypt, where meditation was an important and integral part of people's daily lives.

The anti-aging benefits were recognized by scientists, as late as 1995, when The University of Massachusetts research pointed out that meditation significantly increases the levels of melatonin production. The studies showed that a mere 20 to 30 minutes of meditation can boost the melatonin levels in the blood by almost double.

Melatonin is the hormone, which is basically responsible for sleep, although it also influences the function and production of other hormones in the body. Melatonin is produced in the pineal gland of the brain. According to the Vedas, this is considered one of the seven major energy points/centers or charkas that are concentrated upon while meditating. This particular charka deals with happiness.

There have been experiments where the body clock has been turned back by years; menopausal women were able to bear healthy babies; people suffering from age-related psychosomatic problems made full recovery; menopausal women regained their sexual drive, and fought depression and related menopausal symptoms successfully with the help of HRT.

Science points out that everything in your body is controlled by hormones, which the endocrinal glands produce. Therefore, it would be safe to assume that aging is due to a fast deteriorating endocrine system. The wear and tear that you experience with aging is because the endocrine glands reduce the production of hormones the body needs to stay in the top condition.

The pineal gland deteriorates fast producing less and less melatonin; in the end, you would find that this gland has been completely calcified. With this shutdown, the body loses one of the most effective and efficient free radical destroyers of the body.

Side by side with the deterioration and death of the pineal gland is the decrease of DHEA or the dehydroepiandrosterone, which is a steroid hormone produced by your body. This hormone is responsible for a healthy sexual drive, balancing moods, and keeping a constant body to fat ratio.

DHEA is also one of the key hormones that go after cortisol or cortisone, which is better known as the stress hormone. This in turn accelerates all aging related health problems, such as decrease in immunity, memory loss or impairment, and the inability to right the systems once these have been imbalanced by any type of infection.

Meditation and Happiness

You need to live in the present to be alive, happy, and content. What happened in the past cannot be changed, what might happen in the future is unknown with no guarantee; what you have for sure, yours to use as you want is the NOW, the PRESENT.

According to Buddhist scholar B Alan Wallace, *"We're living in a world that contributes in a major way to mental fragmentation, disintegration, distraction, decoherence. We're always doing something, and we allow little time to practice stillness and calm."*

The Buddhist monks, who believe in this concept, refer to the human mind as *"monkey mind"* because our thoughts keep jumping from one topic to another, just like monkeys jumping from one tree to another.

It looks like living in the present is the only way to stay alive, not only happy. Happiness is a state of mind. It is a way of perceiving and reacting to external stimuli. It is a method where you decide how to react to anything that happens to you. It may seem often that decision is not yours to make, as your feelings steer you to reactive actions.

Meditation Success and Prosperity

What in your opinion defines success? Let us say, you want to be the best in your field, the best mother, the best wife, the best daughter; you want to have enough money, a lovely family, a good house, cars, and in general ,all the comforts that come with today's consumerist life style. Let us assume that you get everything you wished for. Do you think you would be happy?

Success, real success, is when you are happy. To be happy you need to learn to live in the moment. This stage, which is also referred to as *'mindfulness'*, is a state where your mind is intentionally focused only on the present.

When you achieve this state of mind, you are hit by the realization that you are a separate entity from your thoughts, and that you can look, measure, judge, cancel, react, and ignore your thoughts without letting them interfere with you.

You literally awaken to this new experience where you are able to look at yourself with a completely non-judgmental awareness of the present. This state of mind is so powerful, that with just 15-20 minutes of meditation, you can slow down the progress of HIV.

If this is the result when you spend only a few minutes in the 'NOW', imagine what happens when you permanently live in a state of mindfulness.

You are wondering how mindfulness affects professional (and personal) success. Mindful people are able to shed off their insecurities, so they are more content, happier, and more exuberant.

Happy people do not run after the best of life, they learn to make the best of everything they have. As you stop pursuing success and live according to your inner potential, success comes to you willy-nilly.

In this regard, meditation is a paradox. It helps you let go of your goals and instead discover your inner drive and potential; and while doing so, you stumble on the path to success.

Meditation and Grief

Grief is one of the most traumatic feelings of all. Loosing someone precious to you is like losing part of yourself. When a parent, spouse, child, or friend dies, it is common to feel the grief as physical pain. It hurts and it hurts badly. Meditation can help you to cope with your feelings.

But how does it help with grief?

Before you look for answers, imagine the following scenario. Let's say that you live in the USA and you are happy and lucky to have your parents living nearby. You and your spouse are very fond of them and you are in constant contact with them.

Suddenly, they announce that they would like to leave the country and settle in Spain, where they feel they could live a better life. You would be deliriously happy for them, except for the fact that you would miss them terribly, because of one peculiar condition – once they are off to Spain, you won't be able to maintain the close contact that you value so much.

How would feel after their departure? Sad - yes. Would you say you would be in grief? Definitely not! Why? Because, even though while you might never see them again, you can still communicate with them, and you know that they are happy where they have settled, and so you are happy for them, even though you miss them terribly.

Now, imagine that one day – instead of telling you that they are going to Spain, you are told that both of your parents have died in a car accident. Compare your reactions.

Why do you experience heart-wrenching grief in the second case, while only sadness in the first case? The explanation is simple.

The difference is because you know that your parents are happy wherever they are; they exist, even though you are not able to reach them. In the second case, they are lost to you forever.

Meditation brings to you the power of achieving mindfulness, and with it comes the understanding and internalization of the truth that we all are one, part of one universe, one God.

We come from it and go to it; manifestations of life might be different, but life is inextinguishable. Nothing is destroyed in Nature or the Universe; it is only transformed. There is existence after death; life does not cease but changes in its form. Souls do not perish, just the body does.

Meditation has the power of making you believe and feel this from within. Of course, you would still grieve. But you would come to terms with it much faster than without meditation, and your remedial actions would be positive, compassionate, and deliberate (not reactive).

Meditation helps you accept your feelings, come to terms with them and move on by orienting your attention to the NOW. In other words, it helps you renew yourself from within.

Chapter 2 - What Meditation Is NOT - 7 Meditation Myths Debunked

There are a lot false beliefs and myths about meditation, which often act as a barrier for many who would otherwise use this amazing tool to live a healthier, happier, and more meaningful life. Here are some of the most common myths debunked for your benefit:

Myth 1: You Have to Be Religious to Start Meditating

While it is true that religion can play a part with meditation, it is not necessary that you believe in God to start meditating, practice meditation or achieve success with meditation. Most who meditate are spiritual and connect to the Universe.

Meditation is a tool for the mind that teaches you how to look inward and control your response to the world around you. It teaches you that there is no absolute realty, but only the perception of realty from your point of view. To learn to meditate, you need not belong to any type of religion or group. All you need is the willpower and time to practice regularly.

Myth 2: Meditation Is Just a Form of Relaxation

Meditation is indeed a form of relaxation; however, relaxation is only the beginning, the first step in the meditation process. Learning to relax helps you reverse the effects of stress, which is why most stress management classes include some techniques of relaxation that are called 'meditation classes'. It is important to understand that relaxation is just the first step of meditation, and there is so much more that awaits you.

Myth 3: Meditation and Self-Hypnosis Are the Same

This is a myth that is hard to disprove, because there is considerable overlap between both of these techniques. Hypnosis requires relaxation as the first step, followed by a trance where the inner consciousness is awakened and talked to.

Whereas, with meditation, the process starts with relaxation, and is followed by a trance state, where through your inner consciousness, you get to become one with the Infinity.

The difference here is that while hypnosis requires a pre-written script to focus on certain aspect, meditation is a self-discovery journey, where by means of inner focusing you gain a better insight of the Eternal Truth. Hypnosis and meditation **are not interchangeable** terms, nor are they complementary. There is just a slight overlap in the initiation process, but that's where it ends.

Myth 4: Meditation Can Be 'Fast Forwarded'

This myth is often encountered in the West, where the application of technology gives way for people to believe that meditation can be achieved at the press of a button. There are plenty of advertisements that imply this very thing. How often have you heard a promotion where if you play a CD, you will instantly get transported into meditative state. It is doesn't work and you become disappointed.

This is not possible. Meditation is a process that you grow through and with – there are no short cuts here. This is just like going to school; however good the school, you would never be able to condense the curriculum of the 10 years in one week.

Myth 5: Meditation Needs You to Take the Lotus Position

The posture of meditation points to its origin, i.e. the East. This is a place where sitting on the floor with legs crossed is very common and this is one of the reasons why meditation is almost always shown in this position.

However, meditation is not yoga where in order to get the benefits you need to take a fixed posture; it just need you to be comfortable enough to make it easy to focus inwards.

This is why you could sit on a chair, kneel down, or even lie down (though in this position, you might find yourself falling asleep more than meditating).

Myth 6: Meditation Is For Escapists

People tend to think this way because meditation is often associated with another realm of existence. Mistakenly, this sometimes is projected as being removed from realty.

The truth is that meditation not only accentuates realty, but also helps in dealing with all facets of life in a positive and determined manner. From this angle, those who do not meditate would be better candidates for the 'escapist' label as they intentionally close their eyes to the truth.

Myth 7: If You Don't Do It Every Day It's Not Worth the Trouble

Most people believe that meditation has to be done in isolation, every day, and for an exact amount of time. This is not true. Though definitely if would be best for you to meditate every day, it is not strictly necessary. This is not a ritual; it is an exercise that relaxes the mind and body.

Chapter 3 - 8 Types of Meditation

Meditation has many methods, all leading to the one result, Inner peace is found by connecting with the Universe. You can choose any method that suits you best. The description of the following 8 methods can help you decide what feels right to you.

#1 Zazen (Buddhist meditation) Or Zen Meditation

The meaning of the word *"Zazen"* in the Japanese language is *"seated meditation"* or *"seated Zen"*. Its origins can be tracked back to the Ch'an tradition or the Chinese-Zen Buddhism from the 6th century. The principles of this type of meditation come from Dogen Zenji, who is also the founder of the Soto Zen phenomenon during in the early 13th century in Japan.

The Zazen Method

As the name indicates, this type of meditation is generally practiced in sitting position.

How do you do it?

Though the most common form is sitting in the lotus form, it is not imperative to assume that posture. You can sit in any position you feel comfortable following these aspects:

- **Physical aspects**
    - Back should be completely straight from neck to pelvis (in sitting position).
    - Mouth is closed.
    - Eyes are lowered and focused on a spot about 2-3 feet in front of you.

- **Mind training**
    - Focus your mind on your breath going in and out of your nostrils. To help you keep your mind on the breathing, initially you may take the help of counting up to 10, in a rhythmic 1 number per second method.

Is this for you?

This type of meditation is best done in a group of at least 3 people. It focuses on the right posture as a means to achieve concentration.

Those who feel they need a little nudge and encouragement to get into meditation would benefit from this method, as peer pressure would have the meditation form a habit.

Also, the group members could encourage one another to stay on the plan and hence, get into the habit faster.

#2 Yoga Meditation (Any Type)

Yoga is an ancient Indian science that is very difficult to encapsulate in a few paragraphs. The goal of yogic meditation is to achieve enlightenment through self-knowledge. Basically, there are four major types of yoga:

- Yoga involving rules of conduct or *Yama* and *Niyama*
- Yoga involving various postures or *Asanas*
- Yoga through breathing exercises or *Pranayama*
- Yoga through contemplation, i.e. *Samadhi, Pratyahara, Dharana, Dhyana*

Yoga is vast. In fact, it is so vast that you could fill books on each one type. For beginners, yoga posture (*asanas*) and *pranayama* (breathing meditation) can be a good start.

How do you do it?

For beginners here are a few pointers on how to start and where to start. It is highly advisable that you have a *guru* (teacher) or a certified professional if you want to take up yoga as the means to learn meditation.

1. **The Ajna Chakra or Third Eye Meditation** – This method involves focusing your attention on your third eye situated between the eyebrows in the middle of your forehead. The stance is usually in lotus position, eyes closed, looking inwards to the third eye.

   While you focus on that spot, you will find that mind becomes silent. With practice, the "silent time" increases as does your capacity to get to the point where the mind is silent.

2. **The 7 Chakras Meditation** – According to the principles of yoga, there are 7 energy centers chakras in the human body. As you focus on each chakra, you need to say a specific mantra (a specific word) for each chakra. As you complete the seven chakras, you are able to unleash the energy flow through the whole body bringing you to a high level of awareness.

3. **The Trataka (Gazing) Meditation** – This type of yoga involves gazing steadily a fixed object such as candle, symbol or image. You would first look at it steadily, then close your eyes, and try to continue seeing it through the mind's eyes.

4. **Kundalini Meditation** – This is a very method of yoga, but also very powerful. This method aims at awakening the huge dormant energy situated at the bottom of the spine. Without a guru, this could be dangerous to dabble in – so, do not attempt unless you are sure of the guidance of the qualified professional.

5. **Nada (Sound) Yoga** – this type of meditation involves the aid of a soothing sound that will help you move easier into meditative state. From the external sounds, you will learn to move inside and hear the inner sounds of the body and mind. As you progress through this type of meditation, the mind would focus on the "Om" sound that you would be able to project in your mind at will and enjoy the silence it generates within you.

6. **Tantra Yoga** – This is a relatively advanced form of meditation where your mind is directed through contemplation to a type of stillness or emptiness. For example, you may focus and contemplate upon:

   - The gap between two thoughts in your mind;
   - The feeling of complete pleasure or pain;
   - A bottomless black pit or well;
   - The sound of your own heart;
   - A void in your body that is expanding in all directions; and so on.

7. **Pranayama** – This is not meditation per se; but rather a means to get there, and it is an excellent tool to calm your mind and prepare it for meditation. The simplest form and the one that could be almost immediately put to use is the **4-4-4-4 method**. This involves inhaling for 4 seconds (count to 4), holding the breath in for 4 seconds, exhaling for 4 seconds, and holding from breathing in for another 4 minutes.

Is this for you?

Educate yourself about each one of these types of yoga before you decide to take up any one, especially the kundalini, and chakra yoga. For a starting point, use the third eye meditation method in combination with paranayama. Use pranayama as a warming-up exercise so you could train both body and mind for meditation.

#3 Vipassana

This type of meditation originates from the 6th Century Buddhist meditation traditions. In the West, where this type of meditation is very popular, it is known as *"mindfulness."* The meaning of Vipassana is *"insight,"* which refers to the fact that this method involves developing and learning about your body and mind sensations.

How to do it?

- You may sit on the mat or chair, ensuring that your spine is straight.
- Commence with breathing exercises focusing intently on each breath.
- Notice the movement (up and down) of your abdomen as you are breathing in and out.
- As you grow in experience, you may focus on the sensation of the air on your upper lip and nostrils as you breathe in and out.
- As you focus on the breathing, which becomes your primary object, you need to start noticing all other sensations, such as emotions, sounds, smells, etc. which would be the secondary objects.
- As you notice the secondary objects, you allow your mind to linger over it for 2-3 seconds while you label it in your mind as for example, "voices", "feeling", "thinking" etc. No details should be attached to these labels. As soon as you finished labeling, move back to the primary object.

Is this for you?

This is a good way to start because it is well documented, very popular in the West, and so, you will always find a qualified teacher to guide you; and there is a hoard of documents and articles on the subject.

#4 Taoist – The Chinese Meditation

Dating back to the 6th Century the Taoist Meditation is to some extent guided by the principles of Buddhist meditation. The main focus of this method is to focus on the flow of energy within the body. This method is known to not only improve health, but also increase longevity.

How to do it?

The Taoist meditation involves three types of meditation. A brief description of each one follows. For these methods, you need to sit in the lotus position with your spine straight and unsupported. Your eyes need to be half-closed focusing on the extreme point of the nose. For more details, look up the resource chapter at the end of the book.

1. **The Emptiness Meditation** – In this type of Taoist meditation the thoughts are allowed to come and go at their own pace without engaging in any of them. Like a silent observer, you watch the thoughts come and go until you are able to eliminate them all and get the mind empty and silent.

2. **The Breathing Meditation** – The main goal here it to achieve unification of the mind and qi (vital inner force/ energy). There is one instruction – focus on your breath

until it becomes quiet and soft. This is also known as Zhuanqi.

3. **The Inner Vision Meditation** – This method will have you focus on each organ of your body, involving you in a process where you learn about yourself inch by inch. You will need a good teacher or good guide to go through this method – and it is interesting and easy enough to do for a beginner.

Is this for you?

The Taoist meditation is very interesting, but not as popular as other methods of meditation. You may not find enough literature, guide, books or teachers to guide you.

However, if you do, this method is comparatively easier to grasp and master for a beginner than many others.

#5 Qigong

Also known as Chi Kung, this means literally, *"cultivation of life energy."* In ancient times, this method was a secret closed among Chinese Buddhists and Taoist monks/masters. In the 20th Century, it gradually emerged as a meditation exercise set that promotes inner alchemical mode. This method is also included and practiced in Daoist meditation, though it can be used as standalone method as well.

How to do it?

The repertoire of Qigong exercises run into thousands involving as many as 80 different types of breathing. These are roughly divided into three categories. One addresses spiritual cultivation, another is focused on health, and yet another is specific to martial arts.

Qigong can be practiced both in static and dynamic positions, though the exercises pertaining to meditation are always done without movement, sitting down. Here is an example of a Qigong meditation exercise done seated.

- Sit in a comfortable position with your back straight.
- Focus and relax your entire body – your nerves, muscles, organs, etc.
- Focus on your breath; draw in deep breaths, long and soft.
- Focus on your mind; calm it.
- Focus on the portion that is about 2 inches below the navel; that point is known as *"dantien"*. This is where all the vital energy needed to be anchored and pooled.

- Feel the qi (vital energy) surging through your body.

There are many other Qigong exercises such as:

- Embryonic breathing (seated Qigong).
- Microcosmic circulation or small circulation (seated Qigong).
- 8 pieces of brocade (dynamic Qigong).
- Yi Jin Jing or Changing Muscle Tendon (dynamic Qigong).

Is this for you?

This method of meditation requires a teacher in the initial stages. For a beginner this type of meditation is not too difficult with the right guidance. However, a DVD is not enough in the initial stages.

There are many, many exercises; hence, you will get a huge number of choices. Most people prefer the dynamic form to the stationary one.

#6 Mantra

The term *"Mantra"* means *"chant"*. It could be a word, a syllable, or a few lines. It is meant to be repeated again and again, in order to keep the mind from straying into thinking this and that instead of focusing on the process of emptying the mind.

The Mantra Meditation is mostly followed by Buddhist monks, Hindu yogis, Jains, Sikhs and Taoists.

How It Is Done?

- You need to sit with your spine erect, eyes closed, repeating the mantra again and again and again.
- Sometimes, the mantra is aligned with the breathing in-and-out for greater concentration and focus.
- The continuous repetition of the mantra is meant to disconnect the mind from stray thoughts and get it focused within to find the state of pure consciousness.
- Some common and often used mantras are – om, ram-ram-ram, hari om, om namah Shivaye, so-ham and so on.
- The repetitions are normally 108 or 1008 and are helped along by a rosary-type beads string.
- With time and practice, you may be able to hear the mantra in your mind, even if you are voicing it aloud.

Is this for you?

This is definitely a good starting point for beginners as the mantra is an excellent tool to tame the mind into submission. The mantra is also a great way to induce you into meditation, no matter where you are for how much time you have at hand for meditation.

#7 Metta Meditation or Loving-Kindness Meditation

"Metta" means goodwill, kindness, or benevolence. This type of meditation is the heritage of the Tibetan Buddhist monks, who call is *"compassion meditation."* Through this meditation, you will gain self-acceptance, a tolerating attitude, positive outlook for life, empathy, a calmness of mind, and a higher feeling of purpose.

How to do it?

- Sit down in the lotus position or just a comfortable position and focus on generating feeling of goodwill and kindness.
- Start by generating love and kindness to yourself at first and gradually move to others. The progress should be gradual:
    - Generate love and kind feelings for yourself
    - Generate love and kind feelings for a loved one in your family
    - Generate love and kind feelings for a very close friend
    - Generate love and kind feelings for a regular (neutral) person
    - Generate love and kind feelings for a difficult (unkind) person
    - Generate love and kind feelings for all the above in equal measure
    - Generate love and kind feelings for the whole Universe
- The meditation would be aided by specific expressions such as, "feeling limitless love", visualizing sending love to everyone and/ or wishing others peace and love.

Is this for you?

This is an excellent starting place for ALL beginners. However, it is especially beneficial for those people who go through difficult relationships, have low self-esteem, suffer from depression, anxiety, or anger issues; or are feeling unloved.

Buddhist monks advise this type of meditation as the first step towards achieving inner peace and calm

#8 Guided Meditation

Guided meditation is the latest introduction to the modern world. Here, meditation is helped along with specially designed sounds that are supposed to kick the brain waves into the right groove for meditation. This type meditation comes normally in the form of audio; sometimes with video as well.

- **Binaural beats** – First brought to the world by Heinrich Wilhelm Dove in 1839. He found that when sounds of two different frequencies are heard at the same time through different ears, alpha waves are generated (10Hz) which are the waves generated through meditation. In other words, this is a tiny shortcut to help you start. Also there are a number of free audios for guided meditations.
- **Affirmation** – This is a type of meditation that uses imagery to project a certain picture in your mind.
- **Yoga Nidra** – This is meditation along with soothing instrumental sounds or the sounds of nature.
- **Guided Imagery** – This is the method whereby you project a whole scenario in your mind. This is mostly used when healing or relaxation is required.
- **Guided Traditional Meditation** – This is the method where your teacher's voice guides you through the

meditations process, helping you along until you can do it on your own.

Is this for you?

This is advisable for ALL beginners. This is your test drive. It is excellent for improving self-esteem, helping you through grief, and any type of emotional trauma. This type of meditation will get you there almost effortlessly.

It is important that you understand that though guided meditation creates the effect of the meditation and you do enjoy many of the benefits of meditation through it, the best is to go the traditional way.

Chapter 4 - The Starting Point Of Meditation

The beginning is always tough. Like anything new, you need to make an extra effort and be persistent to get into the habit of meditating. The plus point is that it makes you feel good about yourself, about the world around you and about your life. As you advance in the realm of mindfulness, you may experience new things such as:

Visions

As you enter the state of deep meditation, you may experience visions. This is because the mind is relaxing the throwing up the clutter is has collected over the years. If you do see visions, do not be scared. It is normal and it is a passing phase. If nothing else, this is the proof that you are advancing as planned and you are on the way to achieve inner peace.

Hearing Things

Everybody has a strong conscience, but we kind of drown it inside us while pursuing our various goals; especially if what your conscience tells you is not exactly something that matches with your plans or direction. However, as you practice meditation, you will loosen your mind enough to start hearing the voice in your head loud and clear.

Once again, there is nothing to worry about. This is normal. As the mind becomes calmer, the voice inside will grow louder and louder like a real person inside your head. However, as soon as you try to focus on it, it would fade away. With time, your mind will be able to stay still and quiet without any type of noise; yet you will be aware of what your conscience's voice more than ever before.

Sudden Fears

Meditation helps the mind release its emotional baggage. As it is the case with *"spring cleaning"* when you clean your house, a lot of dust will fly here and there. As you are going into deeper and deeper meditation, your old fears about things you would have thought forgotten might surface. Sometimes, you might face new fears that would come as a surprise to you. Do not worry; all that will go away. It is normal occurrence and as you get deeper and deeper, all this would stop.

9 Quick Tips for Beginners

As a beginner you will need all the possible help you can get. You should be looking for tips, shortcuts, little life hacks that would make the transition easier.

We're going to get you started, but don't stop here. Check out these quick tips and keep in mind that meditation like any new thing that is worthy of your effort, will take time and hence, will require your patience, perseverance, and lots of guidance.

Expect Trouble, Be Prepared

Meditation is easy, once you get by the initial, *"Oh God! I can never do this!"* days. But those initial days can be difficult. There can be trouble in sitting still, keeping your thoughts controlled, letting go, breathing, etc. Everything can be topsy-turvy. It is even more difficult if you are a very busy woman – because meditation requires you to slow down. Many have problems with stilling the mind, so just be patient with yourself.

Be prepared for obstacles and troubles. In that way, you would not be tempted to throw in the towel. The good news is that the initial period is not too long and the beginning of your meditation journey can become the highlight of you day and your life. Whichever type of meditation you choose, you will feel the benefits yourself long before they are pointed out to you. You will literally feel like you are blooming, and that's' a great feeling.

Find a Position That You Find Comfortable

You need to find a posture where you are most comfortable and where you can sit with your back straight, eyes closed, and undisturbed for as long as you can. It is as important that you find a posture where you are entirely relaxed. It is also very important that you find a place you can dedicate for meditation.

As you progress with your meditation technique, you will find that the place becomes less and less important, because you will be able to stop whatever you are doing and effortlessly initiate meditation. However, until then, it is very important that you have a place where you feel comfortable physically and mentally.

Use the Stop Watch

Masters, yogis, and Taoists could meditate for days on end without any type of substance other than spiritual substance. However, initially you cannot expect that you will be able to meditate for long periods of time. You could start with as little as 2-3 minutes and build up to 1-2 hours or even more.

Use a stop clock/timer to ensure that the time you are spending is well spent. Increase the time gradually until can meditate at will, anywhere you are, however you are.

Start With Rhythmic Breathing

Whichever type of meditation you pick up, you have to start somewhere. The best point to start, is to learn rhythmic breathing. Learn how to breathe in slowly, deeply and evenly. Not only you will be able to enter the realm of meditation much easier than without, but also learn the process faster.

Use Visualization Whenever You Can

As the mind becomes clearer and quieter, you will do well to start visualizing on your ultimate goal. Gradually, the visualization will pave the way to deeper meditation quicker and with its full benefits.

Use Noting When You Feel Lost

As mentioned earlier, the initial period can be rough; more so if you really want to succeed at it and you put in real hard effort. You will find that your mind will often wander before your time is up – even when the time is relatively short. Do not worry too much about this, as it is normal.

However, be prepared for it. When you feel that your mind is just about to wander start noting things about your breathing. Note when you inhale, when you exhale, how long there is in the in-between time, etc. Visualization is a very powerful tool that you can use to get your mind do what you want it to do.

Yoga for Body and Mind Relaxation

If you are a complete novice to meditation, it would be of immense use to you to first learn yoga. Yoga is a discipline that covers every aspect of your life.

It balances all the systems in the body ensuring that you stay healthy; it also improves body's elasticity to such extent that very soon you would not bother any longer about what posture you need to take. The body automatically gets into the position it prefers most for meditation.

Aim Low and Achieve High

No matter how ambitious you are, do not be tempted to bite off more than you can chew. Just like a baby needs 9 months to be born no matter what intervention occurs, so does meditation require a certain amount of time for you to transcend from novice to experienced level.

Give yourself time and be patient. There are shortcuts, but in this matter, it is best that promise less and delivers more.

Get Into a Habit Groove

It's excellent to develop a good habit. Meditation can be pursued as a habit in the initial stages. In other words, try having a special spot for your home or workplace, playing your favorite (soft) music, burning some favorite incense, etc. This is not compulsory; however, studies show that women who approached meditation as a good habit, found it easier to learn to meditate.

Meditation Tools

Meditation can be enhanced and fast-forwarded using the right tools. Here are a few that you could use in your endeavor to learn and practice mediation.

Music

Use soft and relaxing music, when you start to meditate. Soft music acts as white noise to cut outside sounds from reaching you and at the same time, relax your mind making it easier to focus inwards.

There is special type of music that aids the brain to relax and move inwards. It is often called "meditation" music because it actually promotes that state of mind. It would be music played by a flute, violin, clarinet, etc. Choose something that soothes your nerves and relaxes you.

Sound

You read earlier about the binaural beats. For those who want to cut corners a little, this is your chance. You can use binaural beats to kick-start your journey towards meditation. The binaural beats are part of a concept that has been scientifically proven again and again – and the Internet is full with comments from people who have done it and found it super effective.

Try it and once you get into the groove, you can go back to the traditional ways. Very often, not believing that you can do it, is the biggest stumbling block you face. This short-cut would show you a glimpse in to what meditation can do for you – and once you see that, you are hooked forever.

Candle

It could be a small dot on a wall too. The candle is often part of the meditation as a tool for two purposes – one, it actually symbolizes a higher entity or the Universe, through its wonderful smell and flickering light, which helps you focus your full attention on something concrete.

Initially, as a novice, you likely feel lost and exhausted every time you try to meditate. Add a lighted candle and everything suddenly seems so clear and easy.

Light

It is a no-brainer to say, that you cannot possibly think that you could start meditating in full sunlight. For meditation, you need lowered lights to promote the meditative state without delay. Proper lighting will also put you in the right mood to meditate.

CHAPTER 5 - Yoga and Meditation

Yoga – What is this?

An ancient science that the Indian ascetics practiced for the past more than 5,000 years, yoga is still highly revered in every aspect of modern life. The depth and coverage of yoga is too vast. However, everything that it preaches, teaches, and advises can be divided into 8 concepts:

Yama or the 5 Abstentions

The 5 abstentions are mentioned here in Sanskrit:

- **Ahimsa** – This is the aspect that deals with non-violence. It advices that you should not harm anyone else around you; you need to live in harmony with everyone else.
- **Satya** – This advises complete and total truth/no falsehood.
- **Asteya** - This advises not to steal.
- **Bhamaacharya** – This means that the man had vowed to be celibate or entirely faithful to his wife throughout his life.

- **Aparigriha** – This indicates that you should not covet things that are not yours. You need to focus on non-possessiveness.

Niyama or the 5 Observances

Here the observances are the means to be acceptable and developed in your life:

- **Sauca** – This means purity of mind and body as well as clearness of the mind.

- **Santosha** – This one speaks of acceptance of self, contentment, peace.

- **Tapas** – This means meditation, austerity, and perseverance.

- **Svadhyaya** – This means self-reflection, study of self

- **Ishvava Pranidhana** – This means contemplating on the Universe, God, etc.

Asana

This branch of the 8th path asana refers to the contorted movements of the body she called. The term "Asana" means literally, "a seat". It refers to the postures that could be adopted.

Pranayama or Breathing

This term pertains to the training of breath, which is believed that is synonymous with "life force."

Pratyahara or Abstraction

This part of yoga pertains to the withdrawing the 6 senses from all external objects.

Dharana Od Concentrration

This is about the power of concentration and its applications.

Dhyana Or Meditation

This part involves deep contemplation on the nature of all objects around us.

Samadhi or Liberation

In this path the consciousness is merged with the subject.

Each branch of yoga has further ramifications. To succeed with meditation, you will need to understand that yoga in any form is an excellent base for meditation.

The Importance Of Yoga In Meditation

Yoga is an amazing ancient science that continues to prove to the modern world that the people of ancient civilizations knew much more than the modern man of today.

We have centered on yoga, not because it is the only way that harnesses the power of mind to cure and preserve the body, but because it seems to be the only method that has been thoroughly investigated by the Western world, scientifically.

I hasten to point that Buddhist monks' meditation practices, Taoism, Zen meditation are as powerful instruments for channeling the mind into achieving the seemingly impossible.

The Vedic science boasts that yoga when practiced correctly can cure the body of all the ailments currently known to humankind, including cancer and AIDS. Looking back into the history and documented proof of Vedic medicine and yogic meditation this does not seem too tall a claim.

In fact, I personally advise you to learn 'pranayama,' which is a very simple method of yogic breathing. Check out how you feel after a mere seven days. Your feeling is enough proof of what yoga can really do for your body and mind.

That spiritually yoga can fast-forward the union of the soul and spirit with the Universe, which is no longer contested by the Western world. However, its manifestation or physical changes that it causes in the body are still a matter of debate.

Take for example, the power of yoga to control pain. Yogis do not feel pain. When you read this statement, you are likely to laugh it off as bogus. But, please look back at the previous chapters. Imagine a human being buried alive for 10 minutes – not for days as some studies showed – and think of what would be that person's condition.

Think about yogis sitting motionless for days without food, without sleep, without the need to cover themselves from cold or heat. How do they do it? Meditation, it seems, promotes the production of endorphin. This is a hormone which originates from the at anterior pituitary and hypothalamus endocrine glands.

Endorphins are very similar to morphine, which is one of the most powerful pain-killing drugs available to us today. Morphine is only about 200 times stronger. Since its secretion is more during prayer and meditation, some people call this hormone the "God hormone". Some of the things endorphins do for you include:

1. Bring calm to your mind
2. Control blood pressure
3. Facilitates peaceful sleep
4. Enhances the immune system
5. Controls pain

We have seen that yogis can go without food and even without air. How? As studies (mentioned in previous chapters) show, yoga meditation (and other types) is able to manipulate all the systems in the body, both autonomic and voluntary into a type of physical hibernation while the mind becomes sharper and more alert.

The yogis, when in a trance, are not aware of their physical bodies, but they are aware of their environment. In other words, while they shut off the body, which distracts the mind, so they could use the mind towards self-discovery.

Meditation is able to block pain, shut off all external stimuli such as cold, heat, touch, and so on without causing damage to the body.

For example, yogies who meditates in the Himalayan Mountains, would wear no more than an animal skin to cover their bodies. They are able to exist in temperatures far below zero, without food or shelter without any visible harm to their bodies. How can this be possible? It is, because this is the mind's power at work.

Does Yoga Meditation Change Brain Activity?

Of course, it does. Your body is created in perfect balance with Nature. Your life style, method of eating, sleeping, working – everything leaves an impact on your brain.

Yoga meditation would bring about not only an immense calm and peace, but also the ability to rise beyond the mundaneness of everyday living.

Yes, it does change brain activity because it has been observed that the brain waves change during mediation, the cortex gets thickened and many centers in the brain improve their functioning.

It has been observed that a yogi not only can stop his blood circulation, but also reverses blood flow, reject poison from being absorbed into the blood and feign death.

Yogic meditation is an amazing string of exercises, which trains the brain to accomplish the impossible. You would be able to stop your breath, push your astral body out of your physical body, look into the future, block pain, reverse incurable diseases, and connect with the Universe.

It is amazing what you can do, if you want it bad enough. "Ask the Universe and ye shall receive." The mind is indeed such a tool, with the help of which you can do anything.

Moving Forward From Here

You have made it to the end of this book – congratulations! You have gained great ground in the mystery of meditation and you certainly are now prepared to begin practicing meditation.

This book is by no means all inclusive. The focus was to present to you adequate information to get you started meditating, by providing you with the. most relevant information.

Meditation is a vast topic, and what you have read here is plenty to get you started. Remember, you need to practice, practice, practice, and then practice some more.

I hope that now that you have finished this book, you are feeling empowered by the knowledge about meditation, and that you have developed a desire to begin to meditate and make meditation a part of your daily life.

Stay healthy! Stay happy!

Copyright

Copyright © 2015 by Alternative Imaginings Press All rights reserved worldwide. No part of this publication may be reproduced, distributed, or transmitted in any form or by any means, including photocopying, recording, or other electronic or mechanical methods, without the prior written permission of the publisher, except in the case of brief quotations embodied in critical reviews and certain other noncommercial uses permitted by copyright law.

Disclaimer:

Although the author and publisher have made every effort to ensure that the information in this book was correct at press time, the author and publisher do not assume and hereby disclaim any liability to any party for any loss, damage, or disruption caused by errors or omissions, whether such errors or omissions result from negligence, accident, or any other cause

Made in the USA
Lexington, KY
25 September 2015